Youths' Guidance

Hājj Muhammad Karim Kermāni

Original manuscript name: *Hidāyah al-Sibyān* (in the Persian language) by Hājj Muhammad Karim Kermāni
This Translator and Publisher: Hamidreza Zahraei
Editing, typesetting and design: Ben Pearmain
Research: Sayyed Muhammad Sādiq Mousavi
Email: hamid_zahraei@yahoo.com
Cover Art: Pars Graphic
Printed and bound by IngramSpark
ISBN: 978-0-6450608-0-5

The original author's manuscript has not been found yet, but there are 17 manuscripts of "Youths' Guidance" in the Persian language. One is held in the National Library in Tehran, Iran (ID number: 6868) and others are in some educational and publishing institutions.

All rights reserved. Without limiting the rights under copyright reserved above, no part of this book may be reproduced or transmitted in any form or by any means, electronic or mechanical, including photocopying, recording or by any information storage and retrieval system, without prior written permission of both the copyright owner and the publisher of this book. All work contained herein remains the property of the authors and may not be reproduced without the individual author's consent.

Youths' Guidance

Hājj Muhammad Karim Kermāni

*English translation
by Hamidreza Zahraei*

Acknowledgments

I am gratefully indebted to the Shia Studies research fellow, Sayyed Muhammad Sādiq Mousavi for his invaluable advice, and Publication Manager, Ben Pearmain for his professional paraphrasing and editing.

Many thanks.

Contents

Translator Foreword	9
Youths' Guidance	15
Introduction	17
Chapter 1: In God's Cognition	19
Chapter 2: In the Prophets' Cognition	21
Chapter 3: In the Infallible Imams' Cognition	25
Chapter 4: In Shia's Cognition	27
Translator Comments	31

Translator Foreword

*In the name of Allah, the Entirely
Merciful, the Especially Merciful.
Praise is deserved to Allah (the only God) who
is the lord of all worlds, who is gracious and
kind-hearted, who owns the day of ending.*

Dear young readers, this is a translation of an invaluable booklet written in 1844. The original author was a great scholar who outlined the religion's principles.

As you know, the religion is similar to a building which has a foundation to uphold the top structure. Without a strong foundation, the building is not stable and is unsafe for the person inside it, so the first step in engaging with the religion is to gain the knowledge of its principles by reasoning and thinking.

Historically, there are two recognised ways to categorise the principles of the religion. The first and older category, inferred from the Hadith and Quran by some scholars, has five principles; God's cognition, cognition of the Prophets, cognition of infallible Imams who are the last prophet's successors, belief in the God's fairness, and belief in the Doomsday.

As we see in this category, all of the concepts and principles of Twelver Shiism can not be observed.

Later, the second category was inferred by Shia Scholars from the Quran and infallible Imams' sayings. This category differed from the first category because it contains the complete faith declaration in Islam. In religion, all real believers practically should declare to the unity of God, prophecy of the prophets, leadership of the last prophet's infallible successors, and befriending the believers and hating their enemies. This category consists of four principles, including the cognition of the Shia as the fourth principle. The cognition of Shia means believing the ranks of Shia individuals (such as perfect believers and other believers), loyalty to the God's friends and believers, and detesting their enemies.

In the second category, the element of God's fairness is considered as part of the first principle, which is the God's cognition. Another element is the belief in the doomsday which is considered as part of the Prophet's cognition because in the second principle of the religion we believe in all the Prophet's sayings and that element is one of them. As a result, the second category consists of all beliefs that each Shia individual should declare.

In order to help you understand the author and the contents of this book, I've translated some parts of an article which has been recently written by Sayyed Muhammad Sādiq Mousavi, a Shia studies research fellow in Iran. The article contains some historical events related to this treasure which you will read below, and some comments for more details that you can find at the end of this book.

The author of 'Youths' Guidance'

Once upon a time, more than one and half a centuries ago in Kerman (a city in the southeast of Iran), the city's Sheikh hosted an honourable guest, a scholar famous for knowledge and wisdom. The host asked his guest to write a guide for his young child to learn the right beliefs. The great wise guest accepted and wrote a booklet in the host's house on that dinner party.

The author was Hājj Muhammad Karim Kermāni, a prominent scholar, jurisprudent and theologian. He was born in 1810 in the city of Kerman in southeast Iran. As a child, his great intelligence was noted by his father, Ibrahim Khan, who was eager to nurture his son's gift and provided opportunities for his study.

Hājj Muhammad Karim managed to learn many basic sciences when he was a young teenager and soon surpassed the level of his masters. He didn't limit himself and was always seeking to learn a higher level of education and knowledge. Later on, he met one of the students of Sheikh Ahmad Al-Ahsāei[1] and after hearing

---

1 **Sheikh Ahmad Al-Ahsāei (1753–1826):** A prominent 19th-century Shia scholar, jurisprudent, and theologian. He declared the pure and noble beliefs of Islam, which attracted many scholars and followers from throughout the Islamic world. Sheikh Ahmad's teachings are all based on the Quran and Hadith of Twelver Shiism. He was a prolific writer, he wrote more than 160 books and treatises covering the subjects of theology, cosmology, metaphysics, jurisprudence, interpretation of the Quran and Hadith, alchemy, mineralogy, astronomy, poetry and literary arts, medicine, grammar, and other sciences.

about the great Sheikh's knowledge decided to travel to Iraq to meet him. But unfortunately his arrival in Iraq coincided with the death of Sheikh Ahmad Al-Ahsāei so he was guided to meet Sayyed Kāzim Al-Husaini Al-Rashti [2] in Karbala and found him an ocean of knowledge. He was instructed by Sayyed Kāzim Al-Husaini to get back to Kerman after gaining knowledge to teach what he had learnt.

Leader of all scholars and followers of Sheikh Ahmad after Sayyed Kāzim's death, he wrote more than 240 books and treatises covering the subjects of theology, cosmology, interpretation of the Quran and the Hadith, Twelver Shiism concepts, medicine, math, alchemy, astronomy, and other sciences.

He died in 1873 and was buried in the holy shrine of Imam Husain beside his master, Sayyed Kāzim Al-Husaini, and the Martyrs of Karbala.

After his death, Hājj Muhammad Bāqir Sharif Tabatabaei [3] continued his calling to deliver the pure Islamic knowledge through his books and speeches.

---

[2] **Sayyed Kāzim Al-Husaini Al-Rashti (1793–1843):** Mostly known as Sayyed Kāzim Al-Rashti, is the leading and notable student of Sheikh Ahmad Al-Ahsāei who studied and presented the knowledge of Sheikh Ahmad. He was a magnificent Twelver Shiism's scholar, jurisprudent, and theologian. Sayyed Kāzim Al-Husayni left about 150 books and treatises covering Sheikh Ahmad's doctrine. All the sayings about Ali Muhammad Shirazi (known as The Bāb) being his student is false and slanderous, originating from the devilish and wrong sects of Bābism and Bahāism.

[3] **Hājj Muhammad Bāqir Sharif Tabatabaei (1823--1901):** He was the most significant student of Hājj Muhammad Karim Kermāni, a leading scholar, jurisprudent, and theologian. He clarified his masters' knowledge through a thousand speeches for people and wrote about 200 books and treatises in Persian and Arabic, covering a wide array of disciplines and sciences.

The motive to write this booklet and the history of the youths' teaching

One of the major concerns that affect believers is achieving the right beliefs through the right resources. As the most important issue in their life, they also worry about their children gaining the right beliefs. On that night the host showed concern for his child he asked Hājj Muhammad Karim Kermāni to write a guide about the right beliefs. Although the book was only a few brief pages, it effectively used simple reasons to show the basic features of the religion to young children.

In Islamic jurisprudence, the scholars have considered beliefs as a major focus. They consider practices, such as praying and fasting, as the minor concerns, so gaining the right beliefs is very important in religion. Among all Muslims, but especially Shias, logical learning of the beliefs plays a vital role in religious life. Moreover, it has been mentioned that the heart of the youth is similar to an empty ground that is ready for cultivation so parents have to rush before perverted folks overtake them. Because of this, there are many references in the Hadith that emphasize the importance of youths' education for gaining the right beliefs.

Paying attention to the youths and motivating them to gain knowledge about the religion's principles is obvious in Sheikh Ahmad's doctrine.

Searching through history has revealed a book named Hayat Al-Nafs (Liven Up The Soul). He wrote this to teach young children through simplifying content by teachers. The mentioned book was in Arabic and has been translated by many scholars.

Considering the importance of all this, Hājj Muhammad Karim Kermāni wrote two booklets named 'Youths' Guidance' and 'The Alphabets' for Young Children. At this period, among the contemporary followers of Sheikh Ahmad's doctrine, the wise teacher Hājj Sayyed Ahmad Pourmousavian wrote many books for a variety of age groups, such as 'First Step In Religiousness' in order to achieve knowledge in religion's principles for the youths, as well as some poems for kids to deliver this topic.

Dear readers, you can read the rest of this article at the end of the booklet, which is very helpful to gain more details.

Youths' Guidance

Hājj Muhammad Karim Kermāni

In the name of Allah, the Entirely Merciful, the Especially Merciful. Praise belongs to Allah and peace be upon his worshipers, whom he has chosen.

The sinful worshiper Karim, son of Ibrahim now says; I wrote this booklet, in brief, to instruct the young children in the principles of right beliefs and truths of the knowledge that is the foundation of the sect which has achieved salvation, and to engrave these right beliefs on their hearts.

I also filled it with some obvious reasons for the ones who can discern to gain the benefits, not to accept it only by following, and called it 'Youths' Guidance', including an introduction and four chapters.

Introduction

First, it's necessary to explain some points before stating the beliefs.

You admirable children and chosen darlings should know that your existence in this world is not absurd and useless. It's obvious that you haven't already been in this world, you didn't get yourself out of your mother's abdomen, and you haven't created yourself, so the one that created you and took you out of your mother's abdomen purposely made you for a reason, and has brought you out of your mother's abdomen for an aim. Therefore you haven't been brought into this world only for entertainment, enjoyment, eating and drinking. Hence, try to understand for what reason you have been brought into this world, and where you will be taken to and what you will deal with.

So, like a kind father, I advise you to gain cognition to become wise and acknowledge who has created you and taken you out of your mother's abdomen, who feeds and gives life to you, and finally where you have to be taken to.

Accept my advice while you are still young and your heart is still like a smooth and shiny mirror that hasn't become dim and dull by greed and worldliness, then when you get older you won't feel regret and wish that you had obtained cognition and wisdom while you were young instead of sticking to the entertainment and enjoyment all the time.

Therefore listen and learn what I teach you with all of your attention and your highest level of intelligence, till God forgives you because of being guided and forgives me for the sake of leading you to the right (Allah is compassionate and merciful most surely).

Chapter 1:
In God's Cognition

This chapter is about God's cognition. You dear readers should know that you weren't always in this world. Also, neither were your parents and relatives; someone has brought you all to this world, none of us created ourselves and none of us has brought ourselves here.

It is clear that someone else has got them into this world, someone who is unlike them and that's the God. Thus, no one created God; if anyone created him the God would be a creature like you.

God did not just appear but always has been, always will be, and never dies. If God dies he will be a creature, same as you.

Also be aware that there is one God. If there was another god, same as the only God, then that god should send a prophet towards his creatures to announce his commandment and rule.

However, we have seen that only the one God has done this. He sent his one hundred twenty-four thousand prophets towards his creatures, and all of them came and said that there is one God, and all of them had miracles, which were the reason for their truth. If there was another god, why has he remained quiet and let the prophets of the other God deceive the creatures and make them impious?

Thus because all these prophets said that there is one God, no one offended them and no one made their sayings untrue, and no one ceased their miracles, we recognize that they all have spoken the truth and there is one God.

Moreover, you should know that God is farsighted, insightful, and wise. He created you perfectly in the darkness of your mothers' wombs, complete with accurate organs. Ask yourself, if he wasn't insightful and wise how could he create you in the darkness so well like this?

God has power and strength as well, because if he was incapable and powerless he couldn't create such a huge number of creatures, nor could he make the earth and sky and maintain them. Additionally, you should know that God is not similar to his creatures because if he resembled his creatures then he would be someone like you, so there is no one similar and comparable to him.

Also be aware that there is no partner, co-operator, or deputy for the God to do his acts and duties, he has created this world and the creatures himself. None of the creatures can create someone else, feed someone, give life to someone and take someone's life; only the one God creates, feeds, gives life and takes life for all of the worlds, without any assistance.

In addition, you should know that you must worship this God only and not consider worshipping any other because the one and only God has created you so why would you worship anyone except this God?

Once you settle what I mentioned here in this chapter down in your heart thoroughly then your cognition will be completed, if God wants. About God's cognition, this chapter is enough even for your adults as well.

Chapter 2:
In the Prophets' Cognition

You cherished children now understand that the God has created you then brought you into this world. You should know that when you all came out of your mothers' wombs you were unwise, uninformed and you weren't aware of right and wrong at all and didn't know how you have to treat and behave in this world. Your kind and compassionate God intended to make all the right and wrong clear for you, he desired to teach you how to behave to get your life longer and to avoid struggle, quarrels and being annoyed.

Thus, the God sent one of his creatures from the invisible spiritual world towards you and appointed him as your divine ruler[4] and superior to come down to this world to teach you and to rule among fighting and arguing people. That person is a prophet among all creation.

God has created a divine ruler in every period of time among all his creatures to rule and teach them the right and wrong ways to behave. In total the

---

4 The terminology of "Divine Ruler" in this book is equivalent to "Hākem" in Arabic. The meaning of this word points someone who is a religious and intellectual leader. Sometimes it is accompanied by the official and political leadership and sometimes not (when the God wants an ordeal for people because of the enemies' dominance).

God created one hundred twenty-four thousand prophets among his creation to guide them, and the last prophet was our Prophet Muhammad, son of Abdullah (All blessings of Allah upon him and his family) who appeared in Mecca, had lots of miracles and received the Quran as it descended to him. So be aware he is the best prophet, the best creature, and closer to God than all creations. He has a lot of superior qualities, below are some of his excellences and superiorities which are necessary to know:

You should know that if anyone recognizes the honourable Prophet Muhammad then they will know God, and if someone doesn't know him then they won't recognize God. This is because he's the proof and guide towards God, and no one could manifest the God's attributes like him and never will.

He is the first creature that God created and nothing was created before him. God created him and he was in the invisible world before all prophets then God sent him to guide all creation in the world's last period.

You should know whatever the God gives away and gifts to all creation he firstly gives to the Prophet Muhammad. Then the prophet gives to them because without the Prophet Muhammad people don't have the capability or acceptability to receive these things from God directly. Thus, the God teaches him all the rights and wrongs, then he teaches all the creation, and God gives him all the blessings and gifts then he gives to people and streams all the blessings from his hand. He is the divine benefactor of all and conveys the wishes of all the creation to God because he's the intermediary (mean of blessings) between God and all creation.

He is the prophet of the God among the creation. He is trueborn, truehearted and honest, and he's free of any sins, faults and weaknesses because the

God would never use someone who is sinful, cruel and imperfect to be the divine ruler of his creation. Such a person cannot be trustworthy for the God. Hence what he has said and informed about religion, rights, wrongs, Quran, death, graves, doomsday, assembling and restoring,[5] paradise, and hell are all right and correct. If he was a liar then the God would have invalidated him, would have taken his miracles, would have disgraced him and never let him deceive people or allow them to become irreligious and impious.

What has been mentioned here in this chapter is enough to have knowledge and be aware of the prophet' cognition, if God wishes for anyone to do so.

---

5 The stages after death before entering to paradise or hell.

Chapter 3:
In the Infallible Imams' Cognition

You dear readers have already understood that the God has not created you uselessly and never leaves you without a divine ruler. It is also necessary to understand that after the Prophet, the Infallible Imams must be present in the universe to deliver the religion of the Prophet to all creation, to protect it and to prevent unwise individuals eliminating or changing it. So those Infallible Imams must be trueborn, truehearted, and honest—same as the Prophet—and have to be free of any injustices, faults, weaknesses, and sins. Then people can be sure that what they say about the God's religion is right and what they command is based on justice.

These Infallible Imams own endless excellence which has made them superior to all of God's creatures after the Prophet Muhammad. No creatures can reach their rank and position, and they all have what was explained in four parts above in the prophet's cognition except prophecy.

There are twelve Infallible Imams: the first, Imam Ali, son of Abi Tālib; the second, Imam Hasan, and the third, Imam Husain, were both sons of Imam Ali and their mother was Fātimah, the daughter of the Prophet; the fourth, Imam Zain Al-Abedin was the son of Imam Husain; the fifth, Imam Muhammad

Bāqir, son of Imam Zain Al-Abedin; the sixth, Imam Jafar Sādiq, son of imam Muhammad Bāqir; the seventh, Imam Musa Kāzim, son of Imam Jafar Sādiq; the eighth, Imam Reza, son of Imam Musa Kāzim; the ninth, Imam Muhammad Taqi, son of imam Reza; the tenth, Imam Ali al-Naqi, son of Imam Mohammad Taqi; the eleventh, Imam Hasan Zakiyy al-Askari, son of Imam Ali al-Naqi; and the twelfth, Imam Muhammad Mahdi son of Imam Hasan Askari.

Imam Muhammad Mahdi, who is the king of this era, Imam of the current time and the divine ruler of this period, is beyond the reach of cruel folks and people's eyes. He doesn't see it appropriate to appear among people but soon he will appear then he will judge and rule among all people and eliminate all cruel people. He protects God's religion despite being out of people's sight, he sees all people and does whatever he sees right to do.

After the Imam Mahdi's appearance, all of the imams and the Prophet Muhammad (the God blessed them all) will return to this world, then they will be the king and ruler of the world and make it full of justice. They will bring all the dead people back to life and they will avenge to what all cruel people did. They will be the divine governors in the world until doomsday and will be dominant and ruler on doomsday. They will take all of creation into account and consideration, they will send all the cruel and bad people to hell and all good and faithful people to paradise.

All angels, genies, and human beings are now and will be under their dominance. The divine infallibles will do whatever they wish by God's power in this world and the next world, and they do.

This is enough information to become familiar with the Imams' cognition, if God wishes.

Chapter 4:
In Shia's Cognition

You intelligent youths have already understood that the God never leaves the world without a divine ruler, and Imam Muhammad Mahdi is hidden from the people's sight at the God' discretion. So you should know the God has not left the world without the divine ruler during the non-appearance period of Imam Mahdi, and never will. Thus, the God has to assign someone in every period among these needy weak creatures, someone available for them, someone they can meet and learn the religion from to avoid remaining ignorant and misguided, someone who can judge sometimes at his discretion.

So people can't say in doomsday to the God, "You took the prophet from us and also hid the Infallible Imams, we didn't have any access to them so if we have done wrong that's for the sake of being ignorant!" Hence, for the reason mentioned above, God has assigned among people some of the Shia (Infallible Imams' followers) individuals in every period of time and taught them the knowledge of Infallible Imams.

He has also appointed them among people to be seen so others can learn God's religion from them to avoid ignorance and unawareness.

Those assigned individuals who are the divine

rulers among people are in two groups: the first group is called the Leaders[6]. They possess divine commandment and dominion, and due to their divine permission, power, and strength they hold dominion in the world. Nothing is out of their dominion. This group are the agents of Imams who accomplish their governing rules in this and next worlds.

The second group is called the Nobles. They are not the owners of divine commandment and dominion but they have been granted the knowledge of imams, and they teach the knowledge and religion to people.

These two groups are premiers of people in this and next worlds; in this world, they are divine governors and teachers, and in the next world they are agents and emissaries. The believers will be saved and the unfaithful people will perish by the Leaders and Nobles. By their discretion, they take people to paradise or hell regarding the permission and commandment of the Imams.

Everyone should know the matter of this religion's principle was previously hidden because of ruthless folk's cruelty. No one knew about them but some of their knowledge was among the people only to convey the God's ultimatum[7] to the folks.

Until this time the God wished to reveal their matter at his discretion. The first revelation of this element, which is the fourth principle of the religion, was by Sheikh Ahmad, son of Sheikh Zain-Al Din Al-Ahsāei (God raises his divine rank). The honourable Sheikh revealed this principle of the

---

6 A perfect person who has perfect faith in comparison with others. Perfect individuals are called Leaders or Nobles.

7 A clarified truth which rejects any excuses.

religion (due to the power and strength of the God) to the world and accomplished the God's ultimatum (may Allah reward him of Islam and Muslims, best of rewards for the benefactors). Then after him, Sayyed Kāzim, son of Sayyed Qāsim Al-Rashti (God raises his divine rank) clarified this matter[8]. These two honourable men, by the power and strength of Allah, widened the religion's rules from principles to derivatives on how there wasn't a city that hasn't been reached by their knowledge and cognition. People were examined by these two respected individuals; anyone who accepted their wisdom and knowledge was saved and anyone who didn't accept was deemed to be misguided.

We should know that God has not left the world deserted after them and never leave until the appearance of Imam Mahdi.

Loyalty to them and their friends and followers, as well as detesting their enemies and oppositions, is necessary. Anyone who detests them while knowing of their wisdom, superiority and their faith to the Infallible Imams will be the enemy of the God and the Prophet, a misbeliever, and will be cast out of the religion.

These two respected individuals have spread and widened the meanings of Quran and Hadith in the world. They have said what all Muslims agree on it and they hate any saying, practice, and religion that is against Muslims' agreement. Thus, their

---

[8] After Sayyed Kāzim Al-Husaini, the author of this book Hājj Muhammad Karim Kermāni and then Hājj Muhammad Bāqir Sharif Tabatabaei were responsible to accomplish the mentioned matter.

Dear reader please see the foreword to know about the mentioned scholars also refer to the comments at the end of this book for more details about this chapter.

opposition is the opposition of Muslims' agreement and opposition of Muslims' agreement is impious, and detesting impiety is necessary. Also, anyone detesting while knowing their friends and followers follow them in beliefs is an enemy, impious and misbeliever of Shia religion.

What is mentioned in this chapter about the fourth principle of the religion and in this booklet about the religion's principles, is enough for the youths, if God wishes.

> *Written in one session by the sinful God's worshipper Karim son of Ibrahim, with a desire to please Allah, Allah strengthens us with the steadfast word in both this life and the everlasting life.*
> *Friday night 15 November 1844.*

Translator Comments

Dear readers, the comments below provide further detail about historical discussions around 'Youths' Guidance'.

According to some historical documents in the time of the author Hājj Muhammad Karim Kermāni, some of his opponents changed some words in 'Youths' Guidance'. The purpose of these changes was to accuse him of misleading people. For example, in Chapter 4 of the booklet, he originally wrote "until this time God wished to reveal their matter at his discretion". However, the opponents changed this to "until this time God made them to be known in person". Fortunately, Hājj Muhammad Karim disclosed their falsification in one of his treatises.

It's important to note, none of the four scholars in Sheikh Ahmad's doctrine, including himself, claimed to be a Leader or a Noble. In fact, they always denied this accusation. Moreover, in one of his books Hājj Muhammad Karim Kermāni clarified the topic of "Leaders and Nobles" with three possible manifestations for them. These are being a Leader, a Noble or a Teacher. Furthermore, he mentioned that they don't appear in their leading and nobility attributes in the non-appearance period of Imam Mahdi - although they might appear as Teachers.

He also emphasized the necessity of believing the existence of Leaders and Nobles, not to know them in person. Hence it's necessary to know them as intermediaries (means of blessing) between Imam and people.

Hājj Muhammad Bāqir Sharif Tabatabaei provided further explaination in a treatise about Chapter 4 of 'Youths' Guidance'. According to his treatise, the intention of some sentences in the booklet is not to suggest that Leaders and Nobles, or one of them, should appear among people by their ranks. Although they live among people and interact with them, their specific attribute is unknown. The fourth principle of the religion has been introduced by some scholars before Sheikh Ahmad, but he clarified this principle and provided the insight we now treasure.

I hope this booklet helps you to be insightful and live in a way God wants.

www.ingramcontent.com/pod-product-compliance
Lightning Source LLC
Chambersburg PA
CBHW070304010526
44108CB00039B/1862